General Nathanael Greene Lessons On Leadership

"We fight, get beat, rise, and fight again"

Dominick Morizio Jr.

General Nathanael Greene Lessons On Leadership

"We fight, get beat, rise, and fight again"

© Dominick Morizio Jr. 2016

All rights reserved. No part of this publication may be reproduced or transmitted in any form without the written permission of the author.

The cover image is from an original portrait painted from life in 1783 by Charles Wilson Peale and is now a public domain image via Wikimedia Commons.

Table of Contents

PREFACE 7

INTRODUCTION – AN OVERVIEW OF GREENE'S LIFE AND CAREER 12

DEFINITION 25

CHAPTER ONE – MOTIVATE AND INSPIRE 29

    LESSON ONE - GET SELF AND OTHERS "ON FIRE" WITH BELIEF IN THE MISSION. 32

    LESSON TWO - SET HIGH STANDARDS, BE PRINCIPLED IN APPROACH, AND LEAD BY EXAMPLE. 36

    LESSON THREE - DEMONSTRATE EMPATHY FOR OTHERS. 43

    LESSON FOUR - DEMONSTRATE RESILIENCE IN THE FACE OF DEFEAT, MISTAKES, AND MISFORTUNE. 47

CHAPTER TWO – BE A TEAM BUILDER 53

    LESSON FIVE - SURROUND YOURSELF WITH CAPABLE PEOPLE. 55

    LESSON SIX - UNDERSTAND THE IMPORTANCE OF SECURING SUPPORT FROM SENIOR LEADERSHIP. 65

CHAPTER THREE – GET RESULTS, FOCUS ON EXECUTION 74

LESSON SEVEN - ESTABLISH DIRECTION AND PLAN WITH ATTENTION TO DETAIL, BUT WITH AN EYE ON STRATEGY AND THE BIGGER PICTURE......................78

LESSON EIGHT - TRAINING IMPROVES COMPETENCY AND DISCIPLINE THUS DRIVING EXECUTION. 86

CONCLUSION – "WE FIGHT, GET BEAT, RISE, AND FIGHT AGAIN" 92

BIBLIOGRAPHY 100

ABOUT THE AUTHOR 101

Dedication

This book is dedicated to all those who suffered or died during the War for American Independence and go unremembered today due to the passage of time.

In their own way, they could undoubtedly provide us with many examples of courage, bravery, fortitude, self-sacrifice, and leadership.

Preface

When thinking about a special way to approach a book on leadership, the idea came upon me to marry my interest in history with my experience in leadership, and to present it in an informative and easy-to-read format.

I have a particular fondness for the Revolutionary Period, especially as it pertains to America's War of Independence, but have found the category somewhat top-heavy — with an abundance of books on George Washington, for example. The fact is that there are many lesser-known figures and characters who were instrumental in the States becoming an independent and cohesive nation, and whom we can learn more from and about.

General Nathanael Greene is one such figure and is especially interesting because of the many examples of his outstanding leadership. He also seems more real and human than some of the other figures from the period because he has not been mythicized. In the end too, there is a touch of the tragic in that the hero who had given so much, often putting himself in mortal danger yet persevering through the darkest times of the struggle, died an inglorious death, possibly due to heat exposure, leaving behind ruined finances and a large, young family.

His early death at age forty-four in July 1786, shortly after the war ended, cut his life short and leaves us free to contemplate what role he might have had in the formation of the new nation. This is especially intriguing because George Washington, who became the first President of the United States, considered Greene his most trusted and capable commander.

For example, there is evidence that Washington considered Greene his most suitable replacement if something should happen to himself. Washington left Greene in command of the army in his absence on at least one occasion in September 1780 when, from his headquarters in New Jersey, he went to meet with the French General Jean Rochambeau and Admiral Charles Ternay in Connecticut. The excerpt shows the level of confidence Washington placed in Greene, even to the point of giving him discretion to engage the British if the right opportunity presented itself. George Washington wrote to Greene on September 16, 1780:

> "Tomorrow I set out for Hartford, on an interview with the French General and Admiral. In my absence the command of the army devolves upon you. I have so intire confidence in your prudence and abilities, that I leave the conduct of it to your discretion, with only one observation, that with our present prospects, it is not our business to seek an action or accept it but on advantageous terms."

Greene was a solid tactician and administrator, and above all, very loyal to his commander and benefactor George Washington. He was at Washington's side throughout the war, starting at the Siege of Boston through his time as Quartermaster General during some of the darkest hours for the fledgling American army at Valley Forge. He was eventually given a much sought-after independent command in the Southern theater from 1780 to 1783, and was instrumental in wearing down the British and solidifying resistance in the South, which also led to the events at Yorktown; the surrender of Cornwallis; and the eventual end of the war.

Perhaps due to the passage of time and the changes in language making older works harder to comprehend for the modern reader, or maybe because we are used to the overly brief and quick communication of the internet age, when we read about history, we, the general public, usually do not read the original sources. That is, we read books by authors who have interpreted the writings and events for us instead.

While writing this book, I have developed a deeper respect for such authors and their works, but I wanted to take a different approach and insert, as much as possible, Nathanael Greene's own words to better animate the leadership lessons outlined. It is also my hope that the addition of this small book to the wonderful existing works on Greene not only helps build awareness of his contributions and accomplishments, but also serves to provide inspiration and insight into his leadership for budding leaders.

Introduction – An Overview of Greene's Life and Career

Greene was born into a Rhode Island Quaker family in 1742, as his great-great-grandfather had immigrated to America in the mid-1600s. Greene was a fifth-generation American, and as such, it is understandable how it was possible for him to become a patriot of the American cause early on.

His mother died when he was eleven and his father remarried. The family were merchants in the iron business, and it was through this business exposure that Greene learned many skills that would serve him well in the army, especially as Quartermaster General under Washington.

Greene came from a large family with numerous siblings from his father's two marriages, and he maintained business relationships with some of his brothers throughout his life. Eventually, however, he had to withdraw from the family business due to his wartime commitments, though the family did benefit from his role as Quartermaster General by being awarded contracts for the procurement of supplies. When she wasn't with him at army camp, his wife Caty and their children were looked after and resided with his family in Rhode Island during the war.

Greene walked with a slight limp, the cause of which is not exactly known but seemed to stem from his early years and of natural causes. It was this limp that almost cost him his military career if he had not persevered. In Rhode Island in 1774, he was mocked for it by fellow members of the newly formed militia unit, the Kentish Guards. Greene was encouraged to resign because his fellow Guardsmen felt his limp reflected poorly on them. In a letter to the newly elected commander of the unit, James M. Varnum, dated October 31, 1774, Greene writes:

> "I was informed the Gentlemen of East Greenwich said that I was a blemish to the company. I confess it is the first stroke of mortification that I ever felt

> from being considered either in private or publick Life a blemish to those with whom I assosiateed."

He goes on to say:

> "I confess it is my misfortune to limp a little but I did not conceive it to be so great... I feel less mortified at it as its natural and not a stain or defection that resulted from my Actions."

He also admonishes the complainers for their not having:

> "given me their Oppinions in private than to make proclamation of it in publick as a capital objection.."

We can see that he was deeply upset over what he deemed a natural and almost unnoticeable physical defect pointed out and criticized in an uncalled-for public manner. Not atypical of the times for the gentleman class, Greene apparently felt a slight to his honor.

In spite of the criticism and his initial failure to obtain any officer rank in the unit, Greene persisted, and to his credit, did not resign. From what I can glean in a letter he wrote, his persistence stems from a sense of patriotism for the cause and from personal ambition. He did not resign, but doubled down on his support for the unit. In the same letter, he continues:

> "I would not have the company break and disband for fifty Dollars. It would be a disgrace upon the county and upon the town in particular... I purpose to attend tomorrow if my business will permit..."

What is interesting about this episode in his life is that we get a glimpse of the fortitude that enabled him to be successful in the coming conflict with England. This could have been the end of his military career, but by persevering and mobilizing support, Greene went from being shunned by the Guards to becoming their commanding officer, and he ultimately had a brilliant military career. In the official document from the Rhode Island General Assembly, signed by then Secretary Henry Ward, on May 8, 1775, it is written:

> "the...General Assembly have ordered Fifteen Hundred men to be inlisted and embodied into an Army of Observation, and to be formed into One Brigade under the Command of a Brigadier General and have appointed you the said Nathanael Greene Brigadier General of the said Army of Observation.."

Greene had a thirst for knowledge and a special interest in military matters that started from an early age, so he found his Quaker education limiting in what was permissible to study. In general, the Quakers believed that book learning — other than the Bible, basic math, and basic reading skills — could lead to temptation and sin.

Not only was this a source of tension with Greene's father, but also with the Quaker community at large. Eventually, things came to a head with the Society of Friends in, the

Quaker community, in Rhode Island due to his military interest and involvement with the local militia and Greene was formally cast out of the Society in 1773.

While I did the research for this book and read through his papers, which spanned about twenty-four years from 1762 to just before his death in 1786, it was interesting to see Greene's writing evolve. Certainly, by the time of Valley Forge in 1777, his frequent use of biblical analogies and religious sounding rhetoric, while still in evidence, was well-tempered. I believe that his evolving communication style not only reflected on the reality of the people he was communicating with in his capacity as a wartime general, but also on his increasing distance from the Quaker community.

After the Kentish Guards were formed in Rhode Island, and around the time of their being called to muster in May 1775 to support the militia units engaged against the British in Boston, Greene had met and married Catherine Littlefield. She was about nineteen years his junior, and during the war, she frequently joined him at the army camps. She was a favorite of both George and Martha Washington, not to mention many of the other officers. During the course of their marriage, and often as a result of these visits to camp, Nathanael and Caty had six children together, with one daughter dying in infancy, leaving a large family of five surviving children to support.

In spite of his being given command of the Rhode Island forces sent to Boston, Greene's first taste of battle was actually at this very siege starting in May 1775. His luck continued around this time, since it was during this siege that Congress adopted the troops at Boston to form the first Continental Army. This was also when Greene met George Washington, the first commander of the new army. As Washington and Congress appointed other senior officers, Greene got his second break and was appointed one of the brigadier generals, the youngest of those selected, in the newly-formed Continental Army instead of continuing in the Rhode Island Militia.

After the Americans successfully liberated Boston from the British, and as the war moved down toward New York, Greene had already become a trusted advisor and an important general for Washington. In spite of his being terribly ill during the main Battle of Long Island, and not having a direct part in it, he played an important role in planning and directing the action in much of the other fighting in and around New York in August 1776.

It was during this time that Greene was embroiled in the controversy that followed the fall of Fort Washington. In spite of the Fort's questionable military effectiveness, and Washington's concerns about its defensibility, Greene believed that it could be defended and evacuated in time if need be, and decided to not only hold but to reinforce the garrison. As a result, approximately 3,000 men and valuable stores were captured by the British when the fort fell on November 16, 1776.

This could have been the end of his career, but Greene was able to survive the controversy, largely due to Washington's continued support.

Like the rest of the army and most officers, Greene was inexperienced in war, but Washington clearly saw in him leadership qualities that he knew would blossom over time.

Indeed, Greene had a key role in the soon-to-follow battles of Trenton and Princeton, New Jersey in December 1776 and January 1777. And after these battles, his talent for planning, eye for detail, and experience as a merchant resulted in Washington convincing Greene, very much against his wishes, to take on the staff position of Quartermaster General of the army starting in the desperate winter of 1777 and 1778 at Valley Forge. Greene held this role until October 1780, when he was given an independent command and took over the tattered remnant Southern forces left from the two previous generals, Benjamin Lincoln and Horatio Gates.

His successes in the South, such as at the battles at Hobkirk's Hill near Camden, South Carolina in April 1781 and at Eutaw Springs in May that same year, resulted in bogging down and wearing out the British. The epic cat-and-mouse chase through the Carolinas and into Virginia that played out between Greene and the British General Cornwallis from January through February 1781 was particularly inspiring and helpful for the cause, as it prevented the British from consolidating their control over the Southern States while the war remained stalemated in the North. Greene's successes in the Southern theater led to a train of actions by the British that culminated in Cornwallis's fateful decision to encamp at Yorktown, Virginia, where he was trapped and surrendered to a combined American and French force on October 19, 1781. This was the beginning of the end of the war.

After the war ended, Greene resigned from his command in August 1783 and returned home to his family in Rhode Island. However, his financial situation was very precarious, largely due to poor business dealings and guarantees he made as Quartermaster General. This was in spite of being given land confiscated from Tory planters by the governments in South Carolina, North Carolina, and Georgia, in exchange for his service in protecting and liberating them from the British, plus other holdings he had obtained in the North.

Greene, the retired general and Northern merchant, decided to become a Southern plantation owner and this career change included the ownership of slaves. He settled down at the end of the war with his family at Mulberry Grove, one of the plantations he was given near Savannah, Georgia, and started selling some of his property to pay off his debts.

To me, it is a sign of his desperation that a man who fought so hard for liberty, who commanded soldiers of color during the war and had a strong religious grounding, would so late in life become an owner of slaves.

Around the time of his death, Greene was in intense negotiations with some of his major creditors to restructure his debt. He was working at new business ventures and still hopeful of the coming season on his plantation in spite of some recent setbacks. But before any of this could take root, during a visit with friends in Savannah, Georgia during a period of extreme summer heat in July 1786, Greene began feeling unwell and took to bed in his friend's home; he died a few days later on July 19, at the age of forty-four, leaving his wife and five young children in debt, with no way to fully discharge it. It took years, the sale of their property and help from Congress to eventually free his family from the debt burden.

Greene was a master of seeing the silver lining in any situation in order to persevere. His famous words "We fight get beat rise and fight again" really say it all, but Greene was human and one has to wonder if his collapse came as a result of the accumulated stresses and hardships from the war, combined with new worries from his precarious financial situation and fears over the future well-being of his large family.

Even having a strong and optimistic spirit, none of us can keep up the "fight" indefinitely, and so we must be diligent to groom new leadership. Greene, one of the major contributors to the Continental Army's military success in the War of Independence, passed on and was denied any further opportunities to contribute to the new nation, but we can certainly continue to learn from him. And that, dear reader, is hopefully what we will do through the remainder of this book.

Definition

This is a book on leadership, and since Greene was a military commander, there is a slant toward operational leadership. For clarity, I would like to explain the definition of leadership as I refer to it in this book. An individual who demonstrates leadership has the capacity to *establish direction* and to *influence and align others* toward a common goal. They also have the ability to *motivate* and *commit* a team to action and foster a sense of *ownership* and *responsibility* among the "rank and file" to drive performance.

Operational leadership is leadership that includes all of the items mentioned above, but with a special focus on execution and an emphasis on detail and process. It may at times require a hands-on approach, with one's nose a bit "closer to the grindstone," as the saying goes.

The further down the chain of command in an organization's hierarchy one is, the more relevant operational leadership becomes. That is because these leaders are more focused on execution and tactics versus pure strategy and the posturing that comes along with being a figurehead.

To be sure, George Washington was quite detailed and operational, but as the leader of the Continental Army and a figurehead of the revolutionary cause, he had to be concerned with a broader leadership role. For this, it was often necessary to leave detailed operational decisions to the discretion of his subordinates. This was in addition to the slowness of communication in the eighteenth century, which made delegation a practical necessity.

Besides Greene, there are others who demonstrated outstanding operational leadership throughout the war. One such person was Henry Knox, another leading general, a subordinate of Washington, and a friend of Greene. He must have been an inspiring leader and operationally detailed in order to motivate and direct his men to manually transport a large cache of heavy cannons three hundred miles in fifty-six days — in January 1776, in the middle of winter, from the captured Canadian British stronghold, Fort Ticonderoga, to Boston. This was in order to provide the needed firepower to dislodge the British from Boston. But let us return to our subject, Nathanael Greene.

In the Preface, I provided an overview of Greene's life and career in order to offer the reader perspective for the rest of this book. Should the reader require it, there is a plethora of additional information on Greene available on the internet, in libraries, and in bookstores. For example, one excellent source is the book *Washington's General – Nathanael Greene and the Triumph of the American Revolution* by Terry Golway.

The remainder of my book will focus on select examples of leadership from Greene's career and life, which I believe he especially exemplified and which I hope will serve to provide insight into the following key components of operational leadership:

motivating and inspiring, being a team builder, getting results by focusing on execution.

Chapter One – Motivate and Inspire

The effective leader can rally people to coordinate their efforts and pool their resources to drive outcomes. This begins with creating strategy, then devising tactics and plans that are transmitted via meaningful and relevant communication to the rest of the team.

As mentioned in the Preface, Greene, having been raised a Quaker, had limited formal education beyond the religious, but since he was curious and had a voracious appetite for reading and learning, he found inspiration through his fascination with history — especially that pertaining to the military, with works by the likes of Julius Caesar and Frederick the Great particularly resonating with him.

When we consider Green's leadership aspirations, we can see how Julius Caesar, known for his conquest of Gaul and for how he changed the course of Roman history by usurping power and paving the way for Augustus to become absolute emperor; and how Frederick the Great, who brought Prussia to the forefront of the European powers in the eighteenth century through military and political prowess, inspired Greene.

In an early letter written to his good friend Samuel Ward Jr. from Coventry, Rhode Island in April 1772, Greene says:

> "If we act only for ourselves, to neglect the Study of history is not prudent…. Ignorance when it is voluntary is criminal…"

He goes on to say that:

> "There is no part of History so generally useful as that which relates to the progress of the human mind, the gradual improvement of Reason…

But his next sentence shows where his real interest, and perhaps aspiration, lies as he writes:

"Accounts of Battles and invasions seems to be the peculiar Business of Military Men; and the useful and elegant Arts should be the Study of those who are to Govern the state and form the manners of Mankind."

In this chapter we will draw lessons from Greene in terms of how he motivated himself and others.

Lesson One - Get self and others "on fire" with belief in the mission.

What I mean by getting people "on fire" is igniting their passion and unleashing the energy that comes with it in order to motivate them.

To begin with, a leader has to demonstrate passion for the cause or mission at hand before they can ignite others in this regard. And in order to sustain this passion, it must be genuine and grounded in real belief.

There is an informative book entitled *Business Beyond the Box, Applying Your Mind for Breakthrough Results* by John O'Keeffe, which touches on this concept extensively. In his book, O'Keeffe discusses how it is not enough to be only intellectually engaged, and that we must learn how to harness our passion, "get on fire," and then use both the mind and heart to drive breakthrough results.

Nathanael Greene started his military career because he had an interest in military matters that was grounded in self-betterment. He sustained this interest in spite of his religious upbringing until it grew and found an outlet in the form of patriotic zeal for the cause of American independence. His growing outrage against the British intensified starting in 1774, with the enactment of the Boston Port Act, which was the British government's response to the Boston Tea Party in which they sought restitution for the associated losses. The Intolerable Acts were an umbrella term for a number of acts that the British instituted to crack down on the colonists in the Northeast.

Greene's letters from this time are filled with fiery rhetoric and demonstrate his intensifying patriotism. In a letter he wrote to Samuel Ward Jr. on July 10, 1774, he says of the British government:

> "The Ministry seems to be determined to embrace their cursed hands in American Blood."

And he uses adjectives such as "wicked" and "weak" in describing Parliament. When he thinks of the potential bloodshed in Boston, he goes on to say:

> "O how my eyes flashes with indignation and my bosom burns with holy resentment."

His passion really came to a boil just after the outbreak of hostilities at Lexington and Concord in April 1775, when colonial militia and British troops engaged in brief firefights with casualties on both sides. His zeal is further illustrated by the fact that, in spite of being newly married, he enthusiastically mustered with his Rhode Island militia unit, the Kentish Guards, and set out for Boston to assist fellow Patriots in Massachusetts. To see just how "on fire" he was, while the troops were in transit to Boston, the then Rhode Island Governor Wanton ordered them to halt their march to Massachusetts but Greene ignored the order and continued toward Boston with the intention of joining in the action until he learned that hostilities had settled down. It was only then that he, and the few others with him, reluctantly returned to Rhode Island.

A month later, with hostilities reignited and the Siege of Boston underway, Greene re-mustered with the militia unit and went all the way to Boston. This time, it was different because he did not go to Boston being led, but leading instead, for he had been appointed Commanding General of the Rhode Island Militia.

Learning Summary: Find your passion and get "on fire." Channel that passion into constructive action in support of a cause and take calculated risks to create opportunities.

Lesson Two - Set high standards, be principled in approach, and lead by example.

This is a key quality in an operational leader, precisely because a leader who asks people to do as he does, instead of only as he says, has much greater credibility and finds it easier to effectively inspire and motivate.

Greene, having a Quaker upbringing, was particularly sensitive about the importance of sobriety and also took a disciplined approach in dealing with his troops. During the early part of his military career, during the Siege of Boston in 1775, he was relentless in his efforts to impose discipline on his officers, and thus on his men, and in setting high standards.

In his orders of June 4, 1775, he reminds his officers that there will be training at 5 a.m. followed by prayers at 6 a.m., an apparent mix of practice and piety. In the same orders, he demonstrates an appreciation of the carrot and stick approach to motivation as he instructs the officers to treat the troops:

> "with all the gentleness and Humanity that they Can wish or Expect, but Punish the Refractory and Seditious with Exemplary Punishment."

In his next sentence, he also requests the officers to:

> "Supress... all Debauchery and Vulgar Language..."

In addition to his desire to maintain discipline for discipline's sake, Greene also grasped that the conduct of the troops reflected on their cause. That is, poor behavior would negatively impact local support if the troops acted without restraint and swore, robbed, or otherwise mistreated the local communities they were in. He understood that people would start asking why exactly they were trading the British for brutish fellow Americans. At the time before unity of the colonies, this was especially an issue, as there were many out-of-state troops fighting and parochialism was often evident.

Since there was a public relations aspect to the conduct of the army, Greene had to set a standard and sought to influence his officers and men to follow suit.

As mentioned at the beginning of this lesson, an effective leader must have credibility, and a proven way to build credibility is to have core principles and apply them consistently. Being principled also anchors a team because it provides a compass point for their actions.

One event in Greene's career that illustrates this is when he was requested by Washington to preside over the court-martial of British officer Major John Andre, on spying charges related to Benedict Arnold and the plot to betray the garrison of West Point in October 1780.

Major Andre was captured out of uniform by three militiamen with incriminating documents hidden in the bottom of his stocking. The court-martial tribunal determined that Andre had indeed acted as a spy, and as such, was subject to the death penalty.

It's important to remember that this was an age when personal honor was important, especially for officers and gentlemen, so Captain Andre requested to be shot by firing squad in keeping with a soldier's death, and what he deemed was a more honorable one, than being hung like a common criminal. It is likely that there were many officers in the American army who sympathized with Andre, but for Greene, who applied principle and logic, the way forward was clear. Since Andre was found guilty of spying, there was a predetermined punishment for this offense, and he believed he had no choice but to apply the punishment dictated by law.

However, Greene's real anger was toward the turncoat American General Benedict Arnold, and he wrote of him in a letter to the then Governor of Rhode Island, William Greene, on October 2, 1780, from his camp in Tappan, New York:

> "Nothing can equal Arnolds villainy, but his meanness. He is the blackest of all

> Mortals, and the meanest of all creatures."

A bit of Greene's Quaker upbringing surfaces from time to time in his writings, and he writes of Arnold's treachery in biblical terms. He goes on to say:

> "Since the fall of Lucifer, nothing has equaled the fall of Arnold… and as the devil made war upon heaven after his fall, so I expect Arnold will upon America."

He comment here was insightful because Arnold did go on to cause destruction in the South after this event. It is noteworthy, though, that when discussing Major Andre he seems cool and factual, and uses none of the biblical rhetoric. He seems to have determined Andre's fate based on the events that took place, and not to have made him a scapegoat for his anger toward Arnold. He writes in the same letter:

> "Andre went up to Smiths house; and was concealed two days. He got a pass from Arnold, shifted his cloaths, and set

off for New York by way of Crumpond... Major Andre by the most providential train of accidents fall into our hands, and bring about discovery of this hellish plot. Andree is to be hanged today. The gallows is erected in full view of the place where I am writing."

There was an event in the Southern Campaign during the battle of Hobkirk's Hill near Camden, South Carolina on April 20, 1781, which also serves perfectly to demonstrate how Greene led from the front and by example. At the battle, Greene and the army faced the British commander Lord Rawdon and a few hundred British troops and loyalists. The fighting was fierce and nearly resulted in an American victory. During the action, Greene was right in the thick of the fighting and he likely inserted himself in the frontlines to compensate for a lack of junior officers in the Continental Army at that time.

In the book *Washington's General* by Terry Golway, the author references a quote from one of Greene's aides, Colonel William Davie, in which he says:

> "general Greene exposed himself greatly in this action… so much so, that one of the officers observed to me that his conduct during the action resembled more that of a captain of grenadiers, than that of a major general."

For one of his aides to make a comment like this, Greene clearly had to have been not only noticeable, but also exposed to great hazard and would surely have inspired those around him.

Learning Summary: A leader sets high standards and demonstrates them in his own behavior in order to inspire others.

He has principles and applies them to anchor the team, doing what it takes to get the job done which may entail rolling up one's sleeves and diving into the details in the midst of a problem, even at one's own possible peril.

Lesson Three - Demonstrate empathy for others.

Effective leaders have the ability to empathize with others. This means that the leader can put himself in another's shoes and demonstrate an appreciation for what that person is experiencing. The reason this is so effective is that it builds trust and allows the leader to connect in a meaningful manner. It also helps to break down resistance because the person being shown the empathy will know that he is being heard and understood.

Sometimes the reality of a situation is such that certain action has to be taken regardless of the wishes of the people involved. But for a leader who demonstrates empathy for those affected it can mean the difference between complete resistance and reluctant compliance.

Greene appeared to grasp the importance of the concept, though he seemed to take a practical approach to it. I think this was most probably due to the harsh realities of war and the often desperate state of the Continental Army, especially in the earlier part of the war. But to some extent, Greene may have been impacted by the fact that he was an operator at heart, as operators must be practical in order to effectively drive execution.

During the winter of 1777 and 1778 at Valley Forge, before and during the time Greene served as Quartermaster General, there are two examples that demonstrate his practical, empathetic approach toward the troops and the local population.

In a letter to George Washington written on December 3, 1777, Greene wrote of his thoughts on fighting a winter campaign. It's clear that he had a strong practical grasp of the state of the militia, and of the continental troops at the time, for he says:

> "together with the extraordinary hardships they must be necessarily subject to in the undertaking cannot fail of producing a great mortality, or at least some thousands may be expected

> to fall sick and be rendered incapable of duty..."

From this, we can also tell that he was sensitive to the suffering of the men, and we can see what fighting in the harsh winter weather would mean for them.

In another letter written to George Washington on December 1, 1777, where Greene offered his opinion on where the troops could encamp for the winter, he demonstrates empathy for the local population when he writes:

> "It is said (with how much truth I know not) that all the back towns are crouded with inhabitants; refugees from Philadelphia, if that be true, to turn them out to make room for the Soldiery will bring great distress upon the inhabitants & be productive of no small discontent.."

This passage is insightful because while it shows his concern for the population, Greene's concerns are grounded in the practical consideration of avoiding discontent with the people, so as not to negatively impact support for the cause.

Learning Summary: Demonstrating empathy for others is critical to leading because it drives outcomes by building support and minimizing resistance.

Lesson Four - Demonstrate resilience in the face of defeat, mistakes, and misfortune.

The subheading of this book is a quote from a letter Greene wrote to the French ambassador to the United States, Chevalier de La Luzerne, regarding developments in the Southern Campaign in June 1781. He said:

"We fight get beat rise and fight again."

This single sentence is ingenuous, as it succinctly expresses the entire American strategy of the War of Independence from the beginning, which was to continually field an army and pressure the British into ultimately losing, in spite of Britain's "winning" along the way. What also comes to mind is the popular expression "What doesn't kill you makes you stronger," which has its roots in an essay by the German philosopher, Friedrich Nietzsche.

Greene, who had been in senior positions from almost the very beginning of the war, experienced many setbacks and losses from which he was fortunate enough to be able to learn and mature. As mentioned in the Introduction, one such setback occurred relatively early in the war, during the battles in and around New York, when Fort Washington fell to the British on November 16, 1776. This resulted in the loss of about 3,000 men, as well as crucial armaments and supplies.

While it was not completely of Greene's doing, it was felt at the time that he had primary responsibility for not evacuating the fort. Perhaps Washington had relied too heavily on his advice and judgment before Greene had time to mature. In a letter from Washington to Greene dated November 8, 1776 from White Plains, New York, Washington says:

> "If we cannot prevent Vessells passing up, and the Enemy are possessed of the surrounding Country, what valuable purpose can it answer to attempt to hold a post from which the expected Benefit cannot be had—I am therefore inclined to think it will not be prudent to hazard the Men & Stores at Mount Washington, but as you are on the Spot,

> leave it to you to give such Orders as to evacuating Mount Washington as you judge best, and so far revoking the Order given Colo. Magaw to defend it to the last."

Washington was referring to the two British warships that had recently sailed up the Hudson past Fort Washington as a show of force, but it is clear that he left the decision up to Greene whether to hold or evacuate Fort Washington.

Greene replied in a letter dated November 9, 1776 that in spite of the ships passing by, he believed his decision still served a strategic purpose:

> "Upon the whole I cannot help thinking the Garrison is of advantage—and I cannot conceive the Garrison to be in any great danger the men can be brought off at any time—but the stores may not be so easily removed—Yet I think they can be got off in spight of them if matters grow desperate".

As it turned out, Greene was wrong about being able to get the men and stores out in time if need be. It was a mistake in judgment that could have ended his career then and there. Greene was clearly upset and concerned about the development, as he states in a November 17, 1776 letter, written the day after the fall of Fort Washington, to his friend and colleague Henry Knox:

> "I feel mad, vext, sick and sorry. Never did I need the consoling voice of a friend more than now. Happy should I be to see you. This is a most terrible Event. Its consequences are justly to be dreaded."

However, in a letter dated November 18, 1776, written to Washington from the nearby Fort Lee just two days after the fall, in the immediate aftermath of it, there is no hint of his confidence being shaken or his being overly concerned. In fact, he only cunningly embeds within the letter a vailed defense for his decision to hold the fort. He actually seems to be quite in charge of salvaging what can be saved, and it is a credit to his leadership style that, even in a situation that could have ended his military career, Greene takes the time to commend certain officers and troops that were at the battle. In the letter, he writes:

> "By this account the Enimy must have suffered greatly on the North side of Fort Washington. Col Rollings Regiment was Posted there, and behaved with great spirit. Col Magaw could not get the Men to man the lines, otherwise he would not have given up the Fort. I am sending off the Stores as fast as I can get Waggons."

Perhaps Greene was saved not only by his personal resilience and ability to learn and move on, but by the fact that most of the officers and the army were amateurs themselves, with very little or no military training. They were all learning together, and it was going to be a long struggle. I think too that it was likely Washington and Congress saw potential in the newly appointed General Greene and understood that he had very little military experience or training. What must have mattered greatly in the early stages of the war was belief in the cause, raw talent, stamina, and perseverance.

Learning Summary: It's necessary to keep the big picture in mind, see the forest from the trees, and know what's important. In life, the winner may be the last man standing, not the one who threw the best punches or fired the straightest shots. Mistakes are opportunities from which to learn, so long as they are not fatal. But when you make them, it's helpful to have support from as many members of the team as possible.

Chapter Two – Be a Team Builder

Being a team builder goes beyond recruiting and managing people directly. It has to do with fostering collaboration and building influence in and across an organization. Greene was a rare leader in that he excelled at both establishing a new team and bringing together an existing team to drive outcomes.

More will be discussed on this in the lessons that follow, but I will mention here that an example of his effectiveness at bringing in a new team can be found when Greene took over the Quartermaster Department of the army. He realized that the issues were so great that he refused to take on the challenge and the new position unless his two handpicked candidates were appointed along with himself.

In the case of taking on an existing team, the best example is when Greene took charge of the remnants of the Southern Army. He didn't have the luxury of time to rebuild the team, and to his credit, he did recognize the existing talent and used it effectively to drive outcomes quickly.

Lesson Five - Surround yourself with capable people.

Greene was a walking example of someone who was given an opportunity to lead in spite of his relative young age and lack of military experience, as he had no combat experience and mere months of military training as a militia Private before being nominated in May 1775 as general of the Kentish Guards from Rhode Island. It was in this capacity that Greene commanded the state's troops at the Siege of Boston, where he meet George Washington, and upon formation of the Continental Army by Congress in June 1775, became the youngest brigadier general in the army. Undoubtedly, Greene's personal and family connections in Rhode Island helped him secure his initial position in the local army, but it was most likely his personal qualities and zeal for the cause, and his budding relationship with Washington, that secured him one of the few senior positions in the newly formed Continental Army.

With this in mind, it is completely understandable how Greene appreciated men of talent as much as experience, and how he was effective as Quartermaster General and managed to secure the affections of those he led in the Southern Campaign.

As mentioned above, before he accepted Washington's request to take on the position of Quartermaster General in the winter of 1777, Greene made sure he obtained approval from Congress for the appointment of two top deputies. These were Charles Petit, who served as assistant Quartermaster General, and whom in civilian life was a merchant, lawyer, and politician and looked after the accounts of the Quartermaster Department; and John Cox, who was assistant Quartermaster General as well, and whom in civilian life was a successful merchant and politician. Cox primarily supervised purchases and monitored supplies for the army while he was with the Quartermaster Department.

Greene and his team were able to reorganize the Quartermaster Department and were instrumental in ensuring the survival of the army, especially at Valley Forge during the dreadful winter of 1777 and 1778.

In a letter to Joseph Reed, Washington's secretary, on March 9, 1778 from his quarters at Valley Forge, Greene explains his thoughts on taking charge of the Quartermaster Department, specifically on how to financially compensate Cox and Petit for their roles. The reader may find this unusual and even consider it a conflict of interest, but it was customary at the time for the Quartermaster General and select staff to take a small share of profits from the dealings. We can see that Greene was concerned about his team being fairly and equally compensated, which also demonstrates his grasp of what role remuneration plays in team building and motivation. He writes:

> "I am perfectly willing to share the profits equally with Col Cox and Mr Petit, or in other words I am willing to leave two thirds to be divided as they can agree... that all were equally interested, then there could be no complaints. Col

> Cox and Mr Petit cannot wish or expect any thing more generous and equal than this."

Greene knew that he had a huge challenge to reform the Quartermaster Department and supply the army with sporadic and limited funds from a Congress that had no taxing authority, so he only agreed to take the position if he could secure help from the two individuals who would become his left- and right-hand men. He further writes to Reed:

> "I only agreed to accept the department upon Col Coxes being joind. I would gladly relinquish it to him if practicable, but if not, I am ready to act providing the Col engages.... I wish Mr Petit to engage because I have a great opinion of his integrity."

From this quote, we can tell that Greene thought so highly of Col Cox's abilities that he believed Cox could run the whole department himself, and he singles out a personal quality of

Petit in order to bring him on. It's clear that he appreciated both skill and personal character.

Any senior leader who takes over a company with an existing leadership team can appreciate what Greene faced when he took command of the dilapidated Southern Army in October 1780. I know from personal experience, having been in turnaround situations at two companies, that a leader in this scenario is often met with skepticism, lack of allegiance, and various political machinations.

The leader in this situation also needs time to build credibility while winning over the team and aligning them. It's so hard to do that very often, leaders choose to bring in a whole new leadership team, and possibly some trusted lieutenants.

The associated challenges are all the more complicated when time is of the essence, such as in a turnaround situation. In Greene's case, the challenge was compounded by the associated struggles of operating in a significantly different culture, in an unfamiliar landscape. Greene was a Northerner, a Yankee from Rhode Island, and he found himself commanding a badly mauled army, chiefly composed of militia units and irregulars, in the Deep South.

He also had a morale issue to deal with, since prior to his taking command of the Southern Army, the troops had suffered a monumental defeat under Horatio Gates near Camden, South Carolina in August 1780, on top of prior defeats under the preceding generals Benjamin Lincoln at Charleston and Robert Howe in Savannah.

Greene's success in the South shows just how far his leadership had matured and how brilliant of a leader he was. He understood it was imperative to quickly win the support of key local commanders who had talent, experience, and knew the troops and the terrain. Greene utilized the existing team effectively, only making very selective changes.

When he was contemplating his own logistics in the South, just as Washington did previously in the North when he pressured Greene to assume the post of Quartermaster General, Greene wrote to Colonel Edward Carrington, who would serve as his Quartermaster General in the Southern Campaign, on December 4, 1780, not long after taking command of the Southern Army:

> "On my Arrival at the Army I am confirmed in my Suspicions that great Alterations in the Staff Depart't were necessary. In the Quarter Masters an immediate Change must take Place."

As such, he had in mind to nominate Colonial William Richardson Davie as his Commissary General to assist Carrington. In a letter to Davie dated December 11, 1780, Greene yet again demonstrates his skill at recognizing and appealing to talent. He writes to Davie:

> "you are a single man, and have health, education, and activity to manage the business,... you have an extensive influence among the Inhabitants, and

> are upon a good footing and much respected in the Army."

Other men he came to appreciate shortly after taking command were Henry "Light Horse Henry" Lee, William Washington, Francis Marion, Thomas Sumter, Andrew Pickens, Elijah Clarke, and foreign officer Thaddeus Kosciuszko.

In a letter to Francis Marion, who was a partisan commander in charge of irregular troops, Greene shows his outstanding people skills in starting off the relationship with respect and recognition. He writes on December 4, 1780:

> "I arrived at this Place the Day before yesterday to take Command of the Southern Army. I have not the Honor of your Acquaintance but am no Stranger to your Character and merit. Your Services in the lower part of South Carolina in aiding the Forces and preventing the Enemy from extending their Limits have been very important

and it is my earnest Desire that you continue where you are …"

Greene had clearly made up his mind that Marion would be an important part of his team before he arrived to take command. And the tactics he employed to reach out to Marion before meeting him were spot on. Greene recognized Marion's reputation and accomplishments, and let him know his contribution was not only understood, but also appreciated. At the same time, he established that he was in charge by couching his orders in soft language, telling Marion to stay where he was and continue doing what he was doing. What a brilliant way to assume command.

Learning Summary: When coming into a position of leadership, it's critical to first assess whether you have key people in place whose allegiance you can win and rely on, or whether you need to recruit a new team.

Sometimes the urgency of events will dictate your decision in part or entirely, so it's important to develop the ability to step into a

situation and make the most of the resources at hand.

Lesson Six - Understand the importance of securing support from senior leadership.

In Greene's time, the eighteenth century, it was important to have a benefactor to get ahead. Undoubtedly, he grew to deeply respect and admire Washington, but from the beginning, Greene sought to ingratiate himself with Washington and wound up becoming one of his most loyal subordinates.

I my opinion, the ultimate sign of Greene's admiration for George Washington was the fact that he named his son after Washington, followed later by the naming of his daughter after Washington's wife, Martha.

But right from the beginning, at the Siege of Boston in 1775, when Greene was commander of the Rhode Island Militia, on July 4 and on his own initiative, he sent a letter and a detachment of Rhode Island troops to parade and welcome Washington to his new command as head of the soon-to-be-formed Continental Army. Washington appreciated this show of support and invited Greene for a meeting, thus beginning their close relationship that endured throughout the war.

We can get a glimpse of Greene's thoughts from a letter he wrote to the Deputy Governor of Rhode Island, Nicholas Cooke, from his camp in Massachusetts on July 4, 1775, shortly after Washington arrived to take command. He wrote:

> "his Excellency General Washington has arrived and is universally admird.... I sent a detachment today of two hundred men commanded by a Colonel.... With a Letter of Address to welcome his excellency to Camp. The detachment met with a very gracious recieption and his Excellency returnd me a very polite answer and Invitation to visit him at his Quarters... I expect the general next Day after tomorrow to Visit our Camp."

Greene knew how to foster his relationship with Washington and demonstrate loyalty, but he had a rocky relationship with Congress both before and especially after he was Quartermaster General. Initially, in 1776, Greene had an ally in Congress, fellow Rhode Islander, friend, and father-in-law of his brother Christopher, Samuel Ward Sr. But after Ward's death from smallpox, Greene looked to develop a relationship with John Adams. This relationship soured, though, at the same time his troubles started with Congress over the appointment of foreign officers to the army, and their rank in relation to his and other native officers early in the war.

Considering his ascent to commanding general of the Rhode Island Militia, then to brigadier general in the Continental Army, and in spite of his inexperience, it seems odd that Greene should have made such a public issue out of the rank and appointments of foreign officers, especially before any decision had been made, and before he had fully established himself in the army, to the point of almost losing his position. Two other generals, John Sullivan and Henry Knox, wrote similar letters and were caught up in the affair, but we are primarily concerned with Greene. In a brief letter written from New Jersey on July 1, 1777 to John Hancock, then President of the Continental Congress, he wrote:

> "A report is circulating here at Camp that …. A French gentleman is appointed a Major General in the service of the United States…. If the report be true it will lay me under the necessity of resigning my Commision as his appointment supercedes me in command… I beg youl acquaint me with respect to the truth of the report, and if true inclose me a permit to retire."

The letters caused a big stir among members of Congress, especially since they had not yet made any decisions and they saw it as a challenge to their civil authority. Perhaps a more tactful approach would have been to send private letters to members of Congress, especially John Adams. As such, Adams wrote back to Greene on July 7, 1777 a letter of reprimand, and the sad thing is that the episode more or less ended the relationship between the two men, also leaving Greene without a direct conduit to Congress. Adams wrote to Greene:

> "I never before took hold of a Pen to write to my friend general Green without Pleasure, but I think myself obliged to do it now upon a Subject that gives me a great deal of Pain.... if you or the other Generals Sullivan and Knox, had seriously considered the Nature of a free Constitution and the Necessity of preserving the Authority of the Civil Powers above the military, you never would have written such Letters.. but I really think that a Declaration that you had no Intention to influence Congress... is the least that you can do.... If not I think you ought to leave the service."

In a follow-up letter to John Hancock dated July 19, 1777, and after receiving Congress's resolution on the matter from Washington, which said that the generals were free to resign if they wanted to but that no decision had been made on the foreign officer, Greene explained his position in more detail but stopped short of apologizing. He also backed away from his threat of resignation.

In a letter dated February 9, 1789 to his friend, fellow Rhode Islander and colleague General James Varnum, Greene shares his thoughts on what he experienced in Philadelphia and in the country at large:

> "Luxury and dissipation is very prevalent... When I was in Boston last Summer, I thought luxury very predominant there; but they were no more to compare with than now prevailing in Philadelphia... I dine'd at one table where there was an hundred and Sixty dishes... The Growing avarice, and a declining currency, are poor materials to build our Independence upon."

I believe that at the heart of his troubles with Congress lie three issues: First was Greene's general insecurity when dealing with accomplished and learned men. Remember that Greene, being the son of a devout Quaker, did not have much formal education, and he was keenly aware of this when dealing with the likes of John Adams, for example. This insecurity may have put him on the defensive.

The second issue also has its roots in Greene's Quaker upbringing, specifically in terms of its emphasis on austerity. Greene had little appreciation for the extravagancies of many of those in Congress in Philadelphia, especially when he saw firsthand how the majority of the Continental Army was undersupplied and underfed.

Third, is Greene's proclivity for operations, execution, and zeal for the revolutionary cause. Greene just didn't have the patience or interest in politics, special interest, and the political shenanigans of Congress, especially when it came to getting things done for the army and the outcome of the war.

To make an analogy to the business world, Greene's relationship with Congress would be akin to a senior executive such as the Chief

Operating Officer or Chief Financial Officer having a great relationship with his boss, the CEO or President of the company, but having a terrible relationship with the Board of Directors. The risk is that as long as one has the support of one's immediate boss, and as long as that person is with the company and in good standing, he will be shielded; otherwise he will be out on a limb when something goes awry.

Greene knew how to manage up and ensure the support and confidence of his immediate boss, benefactor, and mentor, George Washington, but he wasn't able to manage the larger relationship with those above Washington in Congress. The risk was that if anything had happened to Washington, or to his relationship with Washington, Greene would have been scrambling for support.

Learning Summary: Make sure you manage up and secure the confidence and support of your immediate supervisor. Make sure not to alienate those above him, as you never know when you will need their backing also.

Understand your tolerance for politics and adjust your behavior and communication style accordingly. Keep in mind that politics are present in every organization and are simply a fact of life.

Chapter Three – Get Results, Focus on Execution

Execution pertains to the putting-into-effect of plans and actions that drive outcomes. It's not enough to have a great plan or idea, or even the best intentions. Outstanding results can only be achieved by way of brilliant execution. In my previous book *How to Drive Operational Excellence, An Integrated and Practical Approach*, I discussed a comprehensive model that addresses the components of brilliant execution.

Brilliant execution is an end result and a manifestation of a cumulative effect. It's about having the right people in the right place doing the right things the right way. Nowhere is this more relevant and more important than in the military, where lives are at stake.

There is no doubt that Greene got things done and achieved results, which means he knew how to execute. Indeed, the lessons in this book have highlighted examples from his career that illustrate some key aspects of leadership in order to execute, such as his ability to build teams. If we keep in mind the poor and lagging communications of the time, the loose political and economic structure of the colonies, and the militia structure of the armed forces, with their limited training, we should be awed by what was accomplished both on an individual and collective level.

Led by Massachusetts, the colonies stumbled into significant armed conflict with the British, starting at Lexington and Concord, with the situation boiling over into the fighting around Boston, especially at Bunker Hill. In spite of the success the militia units had in inflicting causalities on British manpower and pride, it was clear that if the war effort were to carry on in a sustainable manner, a formal and cohesive army would have to be formed. With Washington's arrival in Boston and his nomination as Commanding General, the American effort entered a new phase, with a coordinated effort to put in place the right structure, people, and strategy. It was actually during this time, around Boston in 1775, that we see Greene transition from commander of the Rhode Island Militia to a brigadier general in the newly formed Continental Army.

What was truly remarkable about Washington, Greene, and the other commanding generals of the Continental Army is that they built structure, formed strategy, and executed while learning as they went. The pressure must have been extraordinary, as mistakes could be fatal and wrong decisions lead to annihilation, as the Continental Army was engaged in armed conflict with one of the most professional armies and navies in the world under the British.

One brilliant example of outstanding execution and how far the army had come in such a short time, especially since they had suffered heavy losses and defeat in New York a couple months prior, is the crossing of the Delaware River in the dead of winter in December 1776, and the successful attack on the Hessians in Trenton.

In the action, the Continentals were able to execute a crossing of a mostly frozen river in small boats, with thousands of poorly supplied troops, artillery, horses, and supplies. They marched for miles in separate columns, one led by Greene himself, in darkness to simultaneously descend on and surprise over a thousand Hessians, and then make it back across the same river before being counterattacked by the British.

In the remaining lessons of the book, we will look at two aspects of driving execution: establishing direction and planning with attention to detail, and training to improve competency.

Lesson Seven - Establish direction and plan with attention to detail, but with an eye on strategy and the bigger picture.

George Washington, through his experiences at the Siege of Boston and the battles around New York, saw that Greene had an eye for detail. Therefore, it is not surprising that he turned to Greene to assume the senior staff position of Quartermaster General and sort out the logistical issues facing the army during the desperate times at Valley Forge from March 1777 to a few months before he took on a field command once again in the Southern theater in October 1780.

For a firsthand account of how near-starvation was a part of the Continental soldier's life almost throughout the entire war, the reader can obtain *Private Yankee Doodle, Being a Narrative of Some of the Adventures, Dangers and Sufferings of a Revolutionary Soldier* by Joseph Plumb Martin (edited by George E. Scheer). Martin was an actual soldier in the struggle and at the start of Chapter V on the campaign of 1779, he begins with the following short poem:

> "You may think what you please, sir, I too may think—
> I think I can't live without victuals and drink;
> Your oxen can't plough, nor your horses can't draw;
> Unless they have something more hearty than straw;-
> If that is their food, sir, their spirits must fall –
> How then can I labor with – nothing at all?"

But to return to our lessons from Greene, let's have a look at a September 5, 1776 letter to George Washington written on Manhattan Island, in the midst of the various defeats the army was sustaining there, which serves as an excellent example of Greene's ability to strategize and plan. In the letter, he lays out the options of trying to hold Manhattan Island versus evacuating it. Greene begins the letter with a sober statement of the current situation. He writes:

> "The object under consideration is whether a general and speedy retreat from this island is necessary or not. To me it appears the only Eligible plan to oppose the Enemy successfully and secure ourselves from disgrace."

From this excerpt, we can see that Greene grasped that his troops' current position was untenable, and he was likely aware that he could have exchanged the word "disgrace" for "annihilation." He continues the letter with various tactical facts that support his position:

> "Our troops are now so scattered that one part may be cut off before the others can come to their support. In this situation suppose the Enemy should Run up the North River several Ships... and effect a landing between the Town and middle division of the Army."

Yet Greene demonstrates his understanding of the bigger strategic imperative to retreat, regroup, and carry on the struggle. Survival of the army was critical. He writes to Washington:

> "Part of the army already has met with defeat; the Country is struck with a pannick; any Cappital loss at this time may ruin the cause…. Tis our business to study to avoid any considerable misfortune…"

But the next section of the letter is what I call "Classic Greene," as he again finds the silver lining in the situation. He was a master at making lemonade out of lemons, and he reminds Washington that while the loss of property and New York is unfortunate, it is not a calamity, as New York was primarily a loyalist city. He writes:

> "Two thirds of the Property of the City of new York and the Subburbs belongs to the Tories. We have no very great reason to run any considerable risque for its defence."

And Greene doesn't stop there, since he believes the British should also be denied use of the city. He recommends its destruction and tells Washington:

> "I would burn the City and Subburbs.."

In the letter, Greene demonstrates his ability to see the strategic while considering the tactical, and after weighing both factors, provides a recommendation and a specific course of action. He believes the army should retreat and tells Washington:

> "A general and speedy retreat is absolutely necessary and that the honor and Interest of America requires it."

In another letter to Washington written from Fort Lee, New Jersey on October 29, 1776, Greene proposes the establishment of magazines, supply storage posts, on the route down to Philadelphia from Fort Lee, so that troops will be able to move as necessary between the two strategic points in the coming months.

The letter is informative because it shows Greene's strategic grasp of the need for the magazines and his skill at planning the details. He writes to Washington:

> "Inclosed is an Estimate made of the provisions and Provinder, necessary to be laid in, at the different Posts, between this and Philadelphia to form a communication; and for support of the Troops, passing and repassing from the different States."

Again, we can see his grasp of the strategic and his ability to manage detail. He goes on to consider the price, logistics, and risk of his undertaking, and explains:

> "Should the Estimate be larger than is necessary for the Consumption of the Army, very little or no loss can arise, as Articles will be laid in a season when the prices of things are at the lowest rates; and the situations will admit of an easy transportation to Market by Water."

His recommendation of supplies contains four columns of standard items: flour, beef and pork, hay, and grain. The left margin contains line items such as:

"2,000 men at Fort Lee for Five Months", "At Springfield a Weeks Provision for 20,000 Men on their way to Philadelphia", "At Trentown to subsist 20,000 Men for three months".

For each of these items, Greene lists the required amounts, which means that he must have had assumptions and a specific method to calculate these. For 20,000 men to be supplied at Fort Lee for five months, he recommended 3,100 barrels of flour, 3,100 barrels of beef and pork, 300 tons of hay, and 10,000 bushels of grain.

Unfortunately, Fort Washington fell to the British within a few weeks of his writing the letter, and Fort Lee was abandoned as a result. Though Greene did not see the fall of the forts coming per se, he did cover all angles by ensuring supplies were laid in New Jersey for the army in case of retreat or other action.

Learning Summary: Have a plan and a vision first, then make sure the tactics support that plan.

Keep the big picture in mind and adjust your tactics accordingly and make sure you consider the details.

Lesson Eight - Training improves competency and discipline thus driving execution.

Especially in operational leadership, training is critical to driving execution because it improves competency, and in turn, builds confidence. Imagine yourself standing behind the cash register at a busy fast food establishment, serving customers with little to no training. You might be able to figure out how to pour the beverage from the fountain machine, but you would be very nervous because you wouldn't be sure how to ring up and fill orders. Now imagine that you had three weeks' training. While you might still be a bit nervous, you would have little doubt that you could take and fill an order, and maybe even focus on selling additional items and making recommendations.

The above example is nowhere near as intense as being in a combat situation, where one might lack formal training with high, sometimes fatal stakes. But lack of training is what many in the militia had faced, especially early in the war, and this impaired their effectiveness.

The life of a soldier is not all fighting, which means that soldiers have a lot of idle time, and too much idle time can easily lead to a breakdown of discipline — especially when combined with alcohol, which was common in the eighteenth century. As such, even before Baron von Steuben and the training of the army at Valley Forge, Greene understood the importance of training his troops and the impact proper training had on their effectiveness. This is demonstrated even at the beginning of his military career with the Kentish Guards of Rhode Island in late 1774, and into the Siege of Boston where he led them.

In orders to the troops in his command, written on July 30, 1775 from Prospect Hill in Massachusetts around Boston, Greene demonstrates his approach to driving discipline with a special emphasis on communication:

> "To prevent continued transgressions of orders through please of ignorance,

> general orders are to be read twice to each company... If the troop are ignorant of orders, officers will be answerable."

In additional orders issued on August 11, 1775 from the same place, he addresses disorderly conduct especially from sentries. He writes:

> "Officers and noncommissioned officers to instruct the men, especially sentries, in camp duties. Henceforth, if sentries are ignorant they will be punished severely. Those found pillaging will be dealt with harshly."

In this excerpt, we again see the emphasis Greene places on clear communication and the role it plays in driving discipline.

In a letter to George Washington written on December 1, 1777, Greene says:

> "The health and discipline of troops can only be preserved by constant attention and exercise — we must not flatter ourselves that going into quarters will

> recover the health and discipline of the troops without regard is paid to one and attention to the other."

What Greene is saying is that having adequate food and housing is not enough to ensure an effective army, and that care needs to be taken to keep them healthy. But it is just as important that special effort be made to ensure discipline.

In the same letter, Greene goes on to emphasize the importance of allowing the troops a degree of relaxation, but reinforces the need for driving discipline. He writes:

> "It is absolutely necessary the army should have an opportunity to relax and recover it's spirits—but there is a great difference between constant duty and total relaxation—A proper medium between these two extremes will be found better adapted to restore the spirits of the army and preserve its discipline".

He also demonstrates his understanding of what motivates the troops and why training is important, as he says:

> "Men are naturally apt to sink into negligence without there is something constantly to rouse their attention—The objects of pleasure are so much more inviting than those of Duty that without a restraint is laid on one and a necessity imprest to attend to the other it is ten to one that the objects of Pleasure steal the mind wholly from the discharge of its duty."

Much later in the war, in a letter to the then Governor of North Carolina, Abner Nash, written from South Carolina on January 7, 1781, Greene explains the wretched state of the Southern forces at that time, especially in terms of supplies. Everything seemed lacking: food, clothing, and ammunition — really everything but men. And he explained that without adequate supplies, large numbers of troops were actually a liability because training was not possible and discipline could not be established. He writes:

> "It is in vain to collect large bodies of irregular troops, with the expectation of driving the enemy out of the country; they cannot be long subsisted in the field, nor can they oblige the enemy to fight them, unless it is upon their own terms. Numbers may prevail over discipline, under certain circumstances & in particular situations.... Regular troops are not more brave or better men, than irregular; but as method & order give success in business, so discipline & a knowledge of the tacticks give force and efficacy to an Army."

Learning Summary: As a leader, make sure you build the competency of your team by providing a skills-based and managerial-focused training and insure they have what they need to get results. Maintain discipline and focus by keeping the team engaged.

Conclusion – "We fight, get beat, rise, and fight again"

This quote comes from a letter that Greene wrote to the French ambassador to the United States, Chevalier de La Luzerne, about the general state of affairs of the War of Independence, and entreats him to have France send additional military help, especially land forces. From his camp near Camden, South Carolina on April 28, 1781, Greene refers to "the second division" and writes:

> "God grant the second division may soon arrive and relieve this distressed Country which I am sure cannot struggle much longer without more effectual support."

Greene closes with his famous line, most probably to impress upon de La Luzerne that in spite of it all, the Americans are not beaten and will keep on fighting. He writes:

> "We fight get beat rise and fight again. The whole Country is one continued scene of blood and slaughter."

Not only did I choose this as the subtitle for the book, but I wanted to close with it as well, since I believe it sums up the general strategy employed throughout the War of Independence not only by Greene, but also by Washington. Its sentiment is also a powerful motivator for life in general as it is often full of ups and downs.

I mentioned earlier in the book that there is a bit of tragedy in Greene's story, and while I was reading through some of his final letters from just before he died, I was personally moved by the difficult state of his affairs.

Greene was plagued by a mix of bad business decisions and commitments he had made during the war, compounded by some bad luck and setbacks from his new plantation life. He was selling assets to pay off some of his debt while trying to refinance other portions of it, and he was also seeking out new business ventures to bring in sources of cash flow.

In a letter to his good friend and fellow general Henry Knox, written on March 12, 1786 from Mulberry Grove, Georgia, Greene says:

> "I have been so embarrassed and perplexed in my private affairs for a long time past which originated in the progress of the War that I have but little spirit or pleasure on such subjects... My family is in distress and I am overwhelmed with difficulties and God knows when or where they will end. I work hard and live poor but I fear all this will not extricate me."

In an additional letter written to his other good friend Samuel Ward Jr. on April 4, 1786 from his new home in Mulberry Grove, only two months before he died, Greene describes his situation and debt obligations. He writes:

> "it still hangs heavy upon my spirits as life and lawsuits have uncertain issues. Misfortunes have been hovering about

> me ever since my arrival. I had fifty barrels of Rice burnt soon after I came here and a little time ago I had forty five sunk and spoiled. These two losses... and my Crops falling short... has involved me in a disagreeable situation. And how to extricate my self I know not."

In the same letter, we get a glimpse of that optimism and "glass half full" perspective, which I believe enabled Greene to lead and persevere through the darkest hours of the war. He continues to Ward:

> "Our situation here is pleasant and convenient. The house is large the Garden extensive and elegant. The Trees shrubs and flowers are numerous and beautiful. There is a great variety of fruit Trees which add both to the pleasures of sight and taste.... We are now engaged in planting and if no new misfortunes attack us we have a good prospect of a fine crop."

In this letter, one of the last of Greene's life, the true secret of his success, and perhaps the biggest lesson we can draw, is revealed: Always look for the silver lining to draw hope and strength in order to persevere.

Even with his finances in disarray and a heavy debt burden, which meant a precarious future for his young family, Greene still found hope in the next crop and comfort in the surrounding beauty of his fruit trees.

Likewise, he must have found beauty in the white snow at Valley Forge in the deep winter of 1777 and 1778, as well as hope that the training and drilling being conducted in the army would bear fruit and eventually lead to victory.

In Chapter One, we discussed examples from Greene's career related to motivation and inspiration. Lesson One was concerned with getting oneself and others "on fire" by having a genuine belief in the mission at hand. I stressed the need for one to find passion and to channel that passion into constructive action while taking calculated risks.

In Lesson Two, the need to set high standards, be principled, and lead by example was illustrated by the events of Greene's career. He set high standards and knew how to walk the talk in order to inspire others to emulate him, and his principled approach anchored the troops and set a moral compass. He also did what it took to get the job done and saw the big picture while maintaining a keen eye for detail.

Lesson Three showed the importance of demonstrating empathy for others and how doing so drives outcomes by building support and minimizing resistance and backlash.

Lesson Four drew on examples from Greene's career that expounded the need for resilience in the face of defeat, mistakes, and misfortune. The lesson emphasized how it is necessary to keep the big picture in mind and that mistakes, if not fatal, are opportunities to learn. As mentioned throughout the book, Greene was a master of looking for the silver lining in any situation in order to persevere.

Chapter Two, "Be a Team Builder," consists of two lessons. Lesson Five, entitled "Surround yourself with capable people," discusses how a leader must assess a situation to determine whether the key people are in place and whether allegiance can be gained from the existing team members. It's a vital skill to be able to step into a situation and make the most of the resources at hand.

Lesson Six explains the importance of securing support from senior leadership and managing up, while making sure not to alienate those above one's immediate supervisor. It's important to develop a tolerance for politics, which are a fact of life and present everywhere, and to adjust accordingly.

Chapter Three is about getting results with a focus on execution and leads with Lesson Seven on establishing direction and planning with attention to detail. It stresses the value of having a plan, as well as supporting tactics.

And the last lesson in the book, Lesson Eight, reveals how training improves competency and discipline, which in turn drives execution. As a leader, one has to build competency in a team by providing skills-based training. This will allow leaders to maintain discipline and focus through engagement.

As a parting word to you, dear reader, and in memory of Nathanael Greene: When times get tough in your life, look for the silver lining and remember the General's words to France: "We fight get beat rise and fight again."

Bibliography

National Archives Founders Online, founders.archives.gov

Kentish Guards Rhode Island Militia, www.kentishguards.org

"The Papers of General Nathanael Greene" Edited by Richard K. Showman. Assistant editors, Margaret Cobb and Robert E. McCarthy. Assisted by Joyce Boulind, Noel P. Conlon, and Nathaniel N. Shipton. Volumes 1, 2, 3, 4, 5, 6, 13.

Golway, Terry. Washington's General: Nathanael Greene and the Triumph of the American Revolution" Henry Holt, 2006

University of Pennsylvania archives and records center, http://www.archives.upenn.edu/people/1700s/Petit_chas.html

Revolutionary New Jersey, http://revolutionarynj.org/neighbor/colonel-john-cox/

About the Author

Dominick Morizio Jr. has over twenty-five years of international operations experience with leading companies and brands such as Yum! China, Subway, Domino's, Gloria Jean's Coffees, Boost Juice, and Blockbuster. He is fluent in Mandarin Chinese and thrives in multicultural operating environments. He is also the author of, *How to Drive Operational Excellence, An Integrated and Practical Approach.*

Dominick has a longstanding interest in history with a special concentration on influential military leaders throughout the ages. The author can be reached at **dmoriziojr@gmail.com**

www.ingramcontent.com/pod-product-compliance
Lightning Source LLC
Chambersburg PA
CBHW060359190526
45169CB00002B/664